CLASSIC STORIES OF CHINA

History Stories

Compiled by Song Shuhong

CHINA INTERCONTINENTAL PRESS

图书在版编目（CIP）数据

中国历史故事：英文／宋舒红著；钱清译．
——北京：五洲传播出版社，2011.7
（中国经典故事系列）
ISBN 978-7-5085-2153-4

Ⅰ．①中… Ⅱ．①宋… ②钱… Ⅲ．①历史故事－
作品集－中国－英文 Ⅳ．① I247.8

中国版本图书馆CIP数据核字(2011)第131821号

出　版　人：荆孝敏
编　　　者：宋舒红
翻　　　译：钱　清
责任编辑：王　莉
设计指导：缪　惟
设计制作：苑立静
插　　　图：李思东

中国历史故事

出版发行：五洲传播出版社
社　　址：北京市海淀区莲花池东路北小马厂6号
邮政编码：100038
发行电话：010-82001477
制版单位：北京锦绣圣艺文化发展有限公司
印　　刷：北京天颖印刷有限公司
开　　本：787x1092　1/32
印　　张：5.75
版　　次：2011年8月第1版　2015年5月第2次印刷
书　　号：ISBN 978-7-5085-2153-4
定　　价：56.00元

Preface

China has written history of about 5,000 years. "Chinese history" here refers to the part of the Chinese history form the Xia Dynasty in 2070 BC until the Revolution of 1911 that overthrew the Qing Dynasty (1644-1911), China's last feudal dynasty.

During the prolonged period of time, the Chinese created a splendid civilization, and Chinese achievements made during the period in socio-economic development exerted great influence on the world as a whole.

The long history has given birth to many historical figures and stories related to them. Many Chinese idioms, slangs and sayings are rooted in them. They become the core of China's ancient civilization, and helped enrich the Chinese language, ideology and the way the Chinese behave.

Stories taken in the book are few in number, but are expected to be good enough to help readers learn more of China.

CONTENTS

Xia Dynasty King Jie Brings About the Collapse of His Dynasty

The Xia Dynasty is the first dynasty to be described in ancient Chinese historical chronicles. The Xia existed for over 470 years between 2070 BC and 1600 BC. Altogether there were 16 kings spread over 13 generations.

King Jie was the last ruler of the Xia Dynasty.

King Jie was an infamous tyrant in Chinese history. His real name was Gui or Lu Gui. He was later given the pejorative nickname Jie which means "ferocity". He was a man of great strength. He could straighten a bent iron bar, kill a crocodile with his bare hands and would often hunt and capture bears, tigers and other beasts in the mountain.

During his reign, Jie often made war on vassal states and was extremely tyrannical in his rule. He was a libertine, who sought only enjoyment, ignoring the welfare of the people. He ordered the construction of a palace in Luoyang, which took thousands of slaves seven years to build.

King Jie was a monarch addicted to debauchery, especially in the area of sex. In the 33rd year of his reign, he embarked on a punitive expedition against the Youshi. In order to sue for peace, Youshi presented him with a great beauty named Mei Xi. Mei Xi liked above all things listening to the sound of tearing cloth and silk. King Jie ordered to please her by levying taxes of cloth and silk on the people across the state. Cloth and silk mountains piled up in the imperial sleeping palace. He ordered the attendants to tear them

in order to please the beauty, utterly ignoring the common people who had hardly any clothes to wear.

King Jie was deaf to the wise counsel of good ministers, but promoted treacherous court officials to important positions. Guan Longpang, an official loyal to the state, who advised him to mend his ways, was sentenced to death. King Jie had his four limbs and his head slowly chopped off - an agonizing death.

The only thing that occupied the mind of King Jie was new pleasure and how to savagely oppress and cruelly kill the common people. In his later years, King Jie had no interest in governing the state and instead focused on constructing a wine pool. He called the wine pool his "night palace" and led a licentious aimless existence here along with thousands of men and women. Sometimes, those who got too drunk might fall into the pool and drown.

Under this tyrant, the people suffered great hardship but could do nothing but pray that one day King Jie might be vanquished.

King Jie considered himself the Son of Heaven. Drunk on his immortality, he raved, "The stars in the sky cluster round the sun, while common people on earth prostrate themselves at my feet. The sun in the sky will not die out, and neither shall I." However, history would mark out a different path for cruel King Jie.

As the Xia Dynasty went into terminal decline, the Shang Kingdom in the lower reaches of the Yellow River grew in power. Seeing the indolence and corruption of the King of Xia, the King of Shang Tang was determined to overthrow and conquer him. Tang acknowledged allegiance to the Xia Dynasty publicly, but in private, he began to strengthen his military forces, in the hope that once the opportunity arose, he could go on the offensive against the Xia.

Tang promoted the able and virtuous minister Yi Yin to a very important position. Yi Yin helped him to make thorough preparations mustering good officers and soldiers. They issued a proclamation listing the crimes of King Jie and led an army to attack the capital of the Xia Dynasty.

Hearing the news, Jie led his army to battle. However, his soldiers and generals were in no mood for fighting, especially when all despised their leader. At the first opportunity, the majority of them deserted.

The Xia army was defeated. King Jie together with Mei Xi escaped in humiliation. He was pursued by the Shang forces, was captured and held prisoner in Nanchao. Unable to cope with the indignity and humiliation King Jie committed suicide by leaping from Nanchao Mountain.

The Xia Dynasty, which had lasted for some 500 years, was brought to a terrible end.

King Zhou's Despotic Rule

The Shang army led by Tang defeated the Xia and founded the Shang Dynasty (1600 BC-1046 BC) - the second slave dynasty in Chinese history.

The Shang ruled from the 17th century BC to the 11th century BC, in all about 600 years.

Di Xin was the last king of the Shang Dynasty. He was later given the pejorative nickname "Zhou" meaning "tyrannical and wicked". King Zhou, like King Jie of the Xia ruled so inhumanely and tyrannically that he brought about the collapse of his dynasty. It is a story well-known in Chinese history.

King Zhou was even more debauched and licentious than King Jie. He spent most of his time completely drunk. A large pool was constructed on the Palace grounds and was filled with alcohol. A small island was constructed in the middle of the pool, where trees were planted, with branches made of roasted meat skewers hanging over the pool. This was called the Wine Pool and Meat Forest. King Zhou ordered groups of naked men and women to chase after each other, frolic and perform a dance called Beili in the Wine Pool and Meat Forest. After eating and drinking his fill, King Zhou would ignore all affairs of state and go hunting with his favourite concubine, Daji.

In order to please Daji, King Zhou had the feet of common people chopped off and even had the bellies of pregnant women cut open. To punish insubordinate ministers, he promoted evil, cruel officials to important

positions and, inspired by an idea from Daji, created the "Cannon Burning Punishment". A hollow pillar was cast with copper. Those who displeased the Emperor were stripped naked, tied to the pillar, the inside of which was filled with burning charcoal. They would suffer an agonizing death.

Because of King Zhou's terrible cruelties, many decent ministers stepped forward boldly to remonstrate with him, but those who did so were mercilessly persecuted.

Seeing that the downfall of the dynasty was imminent, his uncle Bi Gan, together with another uncle Ji Zi and his brother Wei Zi, remonstrated with him.

Bi Gan said, "My King, you kill people as you please, so you have lost the hearts and minds of the people. If you lose the hearts and minds of the people, you will surrender the Mandate of heaven. My King I beg of you, please correct your mistakes. "

These words greatly angered King Zhou. He said, "I have heard that the heart of a sage has seven holes. You are a sage yes? Then I would like to see what your heart looks like."

King Zhou ordered that Bi Gan be killed and had his heart ripped out.

Ji Zi immediately resigned and went back to his own estates to lie low.

After that, no one dared to criticize the King. However, he had no idea he was so utterly isolated. The Shang Dynasty was approaching the end of its days.

At that time, a state named the Zhou was growing in power near the Weishui River. King Wen and his son Wu were slowly but surely building up their strength so they could topple the tyrannical rule of King Zhou of the Shang Dynasty.

Grand Duke Jiang Taigong Does Some Fishing

Ancestral name Jiang, given name Shang, and imperial name Ziya, Jiang Taigong lived in the later years of the Shang Dynasty (1600 BC-1046 BC). His ancestors were centuries earlier given a piece of land called "Lu," so he also took this as his clan name.

Jiang Shang was originally a descendant of the king of the Lu State. Later his clan gradually declined in power and influence, and by his time were just common people. From childhood, Jiang Shang worked hard for a rich family to earn a living. Later, he went to the capital of the Shang Dynasty to try to

make a living as a peddler and butcher

Though impoverished, Jiang Shang was always ambitious, and never gave up studying. He became an expert in military affairs and government.

As he grew older, still without having achieved anything of significance he went back to his hometown on the shores of the Eastern Sea, built a thatched cottage, worked a small piece of land and planned to spend his remaining days living quietly near the land of his ancestors.

However, Jiang Shang had never forgotten his own ambition. Though he was 70 years old, he still followed keenly the affairs of state and the welfare of the common people from his thatched cottage. Hearing the news that the Zhou King was rallying able and virtuous supporters to try to overthrow the tyrannical Shang Dynasty, he immediately set out for the banks of the Weishui River on the outskirts of the capital of the Zhou State.

Jiang Shang lived in seclusion on the River. He often went fishing in the Weishui

River, but he would fish in a bizarre way. He would hang a straight hook, with no bait, three feet above the water. Over and over again he said to himself, "Fish, if you are so desperate to live, come and eat my hook yourself."

Passing by the riverbank and seeing this strange scene, a peasant who had come to chop firewood spoke kindly to the old man, "Granddad, I'm afraid that you will never catch a fish in 100 years that way."

Jiang Shang replied, "What I fish for is not fish, but the king."

One day, Jiang Shang finally landed his "big fish." While hunting near the banks of the Weishui River, King Wen found Jiang Shang fishing in his bizarre way. They got to talking and found they had an instant affinity.

King Wen asked Jiang Shang's opinion about the governance of the country. Jiang Shang shared with him his well-thought-out plans. King Wen was impressed and thought that this could well be the sage who could help him lead the Zhou State. He ordered that Jiang Shang be taken in his coach to the court

Jiang Shang was appointed prime minister and given the title Jiang Taigongwang ("The Great Duke's Hope", or "The One of Whom Great Things are Expected by the Great Duke"). With the assistance of Jiang Shang, King Wen led his state into a period of prosperity and built up the state's military power through increased production and the conquering of various vassal kingdoms. After

King Wen's death, Jiang Shang helped his son King Wu defeat the army of the Shang led by King Zhou at Muye. Seeing no way out, King Zhou set fire to his palace and committed suicide.

Jiang Ziya is regarded as one of the greatest strategists in Chinese history, and is honored as the first famous general and effectively the father of military strategy. He attained an officially sanctioned status which approached even that of Confucius.

Fooled by the Lighting of the Beacon Fire

King Wu of Zhou defeated the army of King Zhou and founded the Zhou Dynasty, thus bringing the dark days of the Shang Dynasty to an end. In history, the Zhou Dynasty is divided into two periods - the Western Zhou (1046 BC-771 BC) and the Eastern Zhou (770 BC-256 BC).

King You of Zhou was the last sovereign of the Western Zhou Dynasty. He was indolent and licentious and neglected all state affairs as he spent all his time and energy in the pursuit of decadent pleasure. Ministers who counseled him to administer the affairs of state in a proper way, were punished without mercy. When he pleaded for a minister who had given advice to the King and been punished, a minister named Bao Xiang was thrown in prison and left there years. His family could think of no way to save Bao Xiang, so finally they purchased a beautiful girl from the countryside, and presented her to King Zhou as a concubine after carefully training her. This was just so that Bao Shang would be set free and reunited with his family.

The girl was named Baosi and she was very beautiful and quickly won King You's favour. However, Baosi did not like King You. So she had never laughed once after entering the palace..

King You was infatuated with her and so he ordered that anyone who could amuse the new empress would be rewarded with 1,000 taels gold. Many people went to the palace to make suggestions as to how to amuse her. However, the empress did not laugh even once and they were all beheaded by King You.

An obsequious villain named Guo Shifu said to King You, "To prevent the Quanrong nomads from encroaching on the frontier, we built dozens of warning beacons on Lishan Hill near the capital in the past. If the Quanrong came, the soldiers there would light the warning beacons. Seeing the beacon fires, your vassals all over the land would come to the capital to fight. Now it is peaceful. If we had the beacon lit, those vassals would be fooled. The empress would see the military forces running hither and thither. She would be very amused and would laugh. "

King You had the beacon fire lit as Guo Shifu advised. He sat with Baosi on the gate tower, waiting to see the fun.

Fire blazed from the beacon tower. Many of the king's vassals led their troops to the capital, but found, to their surprise, not one Quanrong solider.

King You sent word to tell those who had come that it had all been a joke to amuse the Empress. There was no danger. They could go home. The vassals were very angry. They were also hungry and tired and had to return home that same night.

King You asked Baosi, "Did you find

that funny?"

Baosi gave a broad grin. King You was very happy as he had finally got to see the smiling face of his favorite concubine. He awarded 1,000 taels of gold to Guo Shifu. On a number of subsequent occasions the King had the beacon fires lit just to amuse Baosi. The nobles grew more and more enraged.

Then one time the Quanrong really did mount an attack upon the Zhou capital Haojing. King You immediately ordered that the beacon fires be lit. However no armies came to his succour. King You and Guo Shifu were killed and Baosi was captured. The Quanrong army withdrew only after setting fire to the capital.

Fearing Quanrong would come again, the new Zhou King Ping moved the capital eastward to Luoyi in 770 BC, thus beginning the time of the Eastern Zhou Dynasty.

Confucius Travels to Various States

    Confucius (551 BC-479 BC) was a Chinese thinker, politician, and educationalist. He was the progenitor of the amazingly influential philosophical system, Confucianism. This great man lived in the later days of the Spring and Autumn Period (770 BC-476 BC). He was a native of Zouyi of Lu State (present-day Qufu, Shandong Province). The formal name of Confucius was Kong Qiu, and he was also called Zhongni.

    Confucius lost his father when he was a child. Thus, Confucius lived in poverty with

his mother. Confucius was a very bright boy and with the support and encouragement of his mother, he did very well in his studies. It is said he learned ritual law from Laotze, music theory from Changhong and Qin-playing skill from Shixiang. Later he mastered many disciples, gave lectures everywhere, participated in political activities and spread his own political thought. To publicize his belief in the power and efficacy of ritual and benevolent government, at the age of 55, Confucius took his disciples to the Song, Wei, Chen, Cai, Qi and Chu, only returning to Lu at the age of 68. During this period, he went through all kinds of hardships and difficulties. He was misunderstood, treated with contempt, and persecuted, but he never changed his beliefs or gave up his mission.

One day, Chang Tsu and Chieh Ni were at work in the field together, when Confucius passed by. He sent Tsze Lu to inquire about a ford. Chang Tsu said, "Who is he that holds the reins in the carriage there?" Tsze Lu told him, "It is Kung Chiu."

"Really? It is Kung Chiu of Lu?" he asked incredulous. "Yes," was the reply, to which the other rejoined, "He well knows the ford."

Chich Ni said, "Are you not the disciple of Kung Chiu of Lu?"

"I am," he replied.

Then Chich Ni said to him, "Disorder,

like a swelling flood, spreads over the whole empire, and who will change this state of affairs? It is better to follow those who have withdrawn from the world altogether?" With this he fell back to his work.

Tsze Lu, who had fallen behind his master, met an old man, carrying across his shoulder a basket for weeds. Tsze Lu said to him, "Have you seen my master, sir?"

The old man replied, "Your limbs are unaccustomed to toil; you cannot distinguish the five kinds of grain; who is your master?" With this, he planted his staff in the ground, and proceeded to weed.

When Confucius and his disciples came to the State of Song, senior officials there plotted to persecute him because they were jealous of his talent. Confucius fled to the place between the Chen and Cai states and lived by eating edible wild herbs. At that time many people did not understand Confucian theory and his way of spreading the theory, so on their trip road, Confucius and his

disciples suffered from many indignities and persecutions.

Confucius was committed to education in his later years. Legend has it that he had 3,000 disciples, among which more than 70 were famous for their erudition. He also compiled the *Book of Songs* and the *Classic of Rites*, and revised the *Spring and Autumn Annals* written by official historians, making it the first historical book written in the annalistic style.

After his death, a record of the words and acts of the central Chinese thinker and philosopher Confucius and his disciples, as well as the discussions they held was compiled into the book *The Analects of Confucius*. Confucius thought and theory developed into Confucianism, which has had an enormous influence on Chinese history over the last 2,000 years.

Emperor Qin Shi Huang

In 246 BC, when King Zhuangxiang of the Qin State died of illness, he was succeeded to the throne by his 13-year-old son Ying Zheng (259 BC-210 BC).

At this time, Ying Zheng was in great danger because Prime Minister Lu Buwei and the Empress Dowager's favorite eunuch Lao Ai had usurped a lot of power. However, the young King had a strong cold heart. Nine years later, Ying Zheng at the age of 21 had ended the domination of Lao Ai. The following year, he dismissed Lu Buwei. Ying

Zheng then assumed full power as King of the Qin State.

Ying Zheng appointed Li Si as prime minister. He also dispatched Wang Jian and other generals to lead attacks on the six other states who were powerful at that time.

Within ten years (230 BC-221 BC), he had vanquished Han, Qi and other states, and had accomplished the unification of the nation. This marks the foundation of the first centralized state in Chinese history.

King Ying Zheng believed that his achievement was greater than that of the mythical Three Sovereigns and Five Emperors, so he should never be called merely "King," but should create a more honorable title fitting to his achievement. Thus he decided to use the title "emperor." He was China's first emperor, calling himself the first sovereign Qin Emperor.

He became the first emperor of a unified China in 221 BC.

Qin Shi Huang abolished the feudal

system of granting land in return for loyalty and service. The empire was divided into 36 commanderies.

He believed a unified country should have unified systems and laws and decrees. Currency, measurements, and scripts that various states originally used should be standardized too. The sizes and types of carts in many states were different from each other. The distance between the two wheels of carriages was standardized to six feet so that road building could be made much more convenient. Perhaps most importantly, the Chinese script was unified. The script of the state of Qin was strictly enforced as the official standard script throughout the land. Thus the state had one language, one communication system for all of China.

Qin Shi Huang ordered the dismantling of defensive works in the border areas between states and built large thoroughfares. Aceess to places like Yunnan and Guizhou Provinces was greatly improved, in order to strengthen land transportation across the country.

Thus black became the colour for garments, flags, pennants. Other associations became standard including north as the cardinal direction, winter season and the number six. Tallies and official hats were six inches long, carriages six feet wide, one pace was 6 ft (1.8 m).

To prevent the Hun tribes from encroaching on the northern frontier any longer, the emperor had the former defensive walls of the Qin, Zhao and Yan states joined into the 10,000-li Great Wall from west to east. Today, the world-renowned structure is a symbol of the long history and time-honored civilization of the Chinese nation.

Qin Shi Huang knew that as he conquered the six states, their clans would inevitably rise again against him. He ordered 120,000 rich families in the country to live in the capital Xianyang so he could control them. He had all the weapons in the country collected. With the exception of those supplied to the army, other weapons were melted and cast into 12 giant copper figures weighing 120,000 kg and a number of enormous bells. His idea was very simple - if those who desired to rebel had no weapons, they would have no chance.

To strengthen cultural control, Qin Shi Huang also ordered all books previously published to be burned. He also had some 460 scholars buried alive.

Qin Shi Huang is a great historical figures. However, his autocracy and atrocities brought great calamity to the people many of whom died in the turmoil. The emperor died during one of his tours of Eastern China in 210 BC (Julian Calendar). Several years after his death, a large-scale farmers' revolt erupted. The unified country that Qin Shi Huang believed would last for eternity had lasted only two generations.

The Songs of Chu Used against the Soldiers of Chu

In 209 BC, when the second Emperor of the Qin Dynasty (221 BC-206 BC) had just ascended the throne, peasant uprisings led by Chen Sheng and Wu Guang broke out. The Qin Dynasty fell into chaos. The fortunes of the rebel armies rose and fell as circumstances changed but gradually, two outstanding leaders emerged - Liu Bang and Xiang Yu.

Liu Bang and Xiang Yu were the most important leaders in the revolt against the Qin Dynasty. As the Qin Dynasty hurtled towards oblivion, they began to fight each other from about 206 BC. The war between the Chu and Han lasted for four years. The army of Xiang Yu suffered a number of setbacks. In 202 BC, the army of Xiang Yu arrived at Gaixia (present-day Lingbi in Anhui Province), but they were closely followed and besieged by the army of Liu Bang. The grain available to Xiang Yu's army was all but gone, and the morale of the Chu soldiers sunk very low.

To demoralise the Chu soldiers even more, Liu Bang sent people to sing Chu songs in area close to the Chu camps at night. The songs could be heard in the Chu camps from all sides.

Hearing the Chu songs, Xiang Yu and his soldiers were shocked, immediately thinking that the Han troops had overrun their homeland and had taken many of their kinsmen captive. The songs also made the Chu soldiers feel very homesick, and more and more of them began to desert and head for home.

Xiang Yu was vexed and found it very

difficult to fall asleep. To help him sleep, he drank wine with his favorite concubine Lady Yu who loved him deeply. The great hero had come to a dead end. Xiang Yu couldn't conceal his desolation, and he sang piteously,

"My strength has moved mountains and my ambition shook the world,

but the times are against me and my steed gallops no more.

What can I do when my steed gallops no more?

Oh what can I do for you now, Lady Yu, my love?"

Lady Yu was moved to tears. She answered her lord with a song,

"Our foes have overrun our land,

from all around they sing our songs.

With such mighty strength my lord can't stand,

what can such a frail woman as I do!"

No sooner had she finished her song than Lady Yu committed suicide with a sword. Xiang Yu was overwhelmed with grief. He led

800 mounted soldiers in a desperate attempt to break through the siege. When they finally retreated to the Wujiang River, there were only 28 of them left.

Hearing that the army of Xiang Yu had been defeated, the leader of the area beside the Wujiang River brought a boat to wait for him by the riverside. He said to Xiang Yu, "Though the area east of the lower reaches

四面楚歌

The Songs of Chu Used against the Soldiers of Chu

of the Yangtze River is small, it extends for over 500 km and has a population of several hundred thousand. If you make this your base, you can still rightly term yourself a lord. Please take boat, my lord. There is only my boat here. Even if the Han soldiers come, there is no way for them to cross the river."

Xiang Yu smiled and said, "Since Heaven has chosen to destroy me, there is no need for me to cross the river. I led 8,000 men in a fight for glory and territory, and none of them survive today. Even if others could honor me as a lord, I could never face them."

Xiang Yu entrusted the steed which had accompanied him for years to the boatman. He led his remaining 28 warriors on foot to meet the Han soldiers who were pursuing them.

The Chu and Han troops fought hand-to-hand. Xiang Yu killed several hundred Han soldiers and suffered more than ten wounds before cutting his own throat.

Liu Bang finally conquered the area east of the lower reaches of the Yangtze River and established the Han Dynasty (206 BC-220 AD).

Zhang Qian's Diplomatic Mission to the Western Regions

In 140 BC, Han Emperor Jingdi Liu Qi died, and his son Liu Che succeeded him. He became known as the Han Emperor Wu.

Once the young and aggressive Emperor Wu (who reigned from 140 BC-87 BC) ascended the throne, he was determined to resolve for once and for all the conflict with the Huns which had lasted for years. At that time, the Hun state was prosperous. Though it was related to the Han Dynasty (206 BC-220 AD) through marriage, encroachments on Han territory were still not uncommon.

At that time, a state called Dayuezhi was being harassed by the Hun and they were eager for an opportunity to strike back. Emperor Wu issued a decree aimed at recruiting warriors to join up with the Dayuezhi in the Western Regions to deal decisively with the Hun.

In 138 BC, an official of the emperor called Zhang Qian (c. 164 BC-114 BC) and a Hun called Tangyifu led a group of 100-odd people from Chang'an on a diplomatic mission to the Western Regions to make contact with the Dayuezhi State.

To reach Dayuezhi, they had to pass by the territory of the Hun. Though they were extremely careful, the diplomatic mission was still intercepted by the Huns. Zhang Qian and his entourage were detained by the Huns for over ten years.

During this period, Zhang Qian never forgot his mission. Even after he got married and had children under pressure from the Huns, he still maintained his loyalty to the Han Dynasty and tried to escape all the time.

Finally, Zhang Qian manged to escape from the Hun and went westward to a state called Dawan.

Since Dawan was a near neighbor of the Hun, the local people in Dawan knew the Hun language. Zhang Qian and Tangyifu impressed the Dawan people with their accounts of the prosperity of the Han Dynasty.

The state welcomed them and escorted them to Dayuezhi.

However, over ten years had passed. The Dayuezhi State which previously had harbored great enmity for the Hun had already settled by Balkh and were unwilling to rise again to fight against the Huns. Zhang Qian and Tangyifu stayed one year in Dayuezhi but achieved nothing. So, they had to return.

On the way back, they were detained once more by the Huns. Luckily, the Hun state at that time was beset by civil strife. Making the most of the opportunity, they managed to escaped back to the Han territory.

Zhang Qian and Tangyifu returned 13 years after they had departed on their mission.

In the 20 years after their return, the army of the Han Dynasty embarked on many westward military expeditions, driving the Huns further north all the time.

In 119 BC, Zhang Qian led 300 warriors to the Western Regions on another diplomatic mission. This time they took more than 600

horses, over ten thousand sheep and other livestock and a large amount of gold. They went to the Wusun State to try to persuade them to fight together against the Huns. Though the King of Wusun supported the Han, he was fearful of the Hun, so he was hesitant. Zhang Qian also sent emissaries to Dawan and Dayuezhi, but these overtures also failed. In 115 BC, Zhang Qian returned to the Han capital and was made Prefect of the Grand March. The following year, he passed away.

Originally, Emperor Wu had sent Zhang Qian to the Western Regions for a military purpose. However, after the route to the Western Regions had opened, diplomatic and trade missions became even more important.

On his diplomatic mission to the Western Regions, Zhang Qian opened the way from the Han hinterlands towards the fertile lands of Central Asia. The route extended from Chang'an to Dunhuang in Gansu and then on to the states of Europe and Asia. This route connecting China and the western lands would become world famous as the Silk Road.

Sima Qian Writes 'The Records of the Grand Historian'

Sima Tan, the father of Sima Qian (c. 145 BC-87 BC) , was an official who had responsibility for astronomy and calendars as well as imperial books during the reign of Emperor Wu (156 BC-87 BC) of the Han Dynasty (206 BC-220 AD). His grand ambition however was always to compile a general history. Unfortunately he died before he could start writing it. Sima Qian determined to carry out the unfinished wish of his father. After he succeeded to his father's post, he began to read all imperial literature, to collect and collate all relevant materials and even to go out to carry out field surveys, all in preliminary preparation for the great magnum opus. In about 104 BC, Sima Qian began to write *The Records of the Grand Historian*.

In 99 BC, a great event happened in the Han Dynasty and Sima Qian was intimately involved. This event came very close to aborting the great historical project before it had really started.

Emperor Wu sent General Li Guangli to attack the Hun, who were duly annihalated. General Li Ling led 5,000 soldiers against the Huns, but was besieged by some 30,000 of the enemy. After fierce combat, Li Ling and his soldiers killed more than 5,000 Hun cavalry. However, they were outnumbered and there were no reinforcement on the way, so Li Ling had no choice but to surrender to the Hun.

Emperor Wu imprisoned the mother, wife and children of Li Ling and threatened to punish them. All the officials in the court condemned Li Ling for being so afraid of honorable death and surrendering to the enemy. No one was willing to speak up for Li Ling.

Sima Qian couldn't bear to see this and he stood up bravely to speak. He said, "Li Ling is loyal and filial. He is faithful to his friends and is modest about his accomplishments. In particular, he looks after his soldiers well and always personally leads the battle charge. He surrendered because he had no choice: he was driven from pillar to post. The reason why he didn't choose to die by suicide is that he wants to live in the hope of rendering future service to the Han Dynasty."

Emperor Wu was extremely angry at these words, thinking that Sima Qian was denouncing General Li Guangli who was the elder brother of the emperor's favorite concubine.

The emperor put Sima Qian in prison and sent some officials to interrogate and torture him. Sima Qian stood bravely resolute despite the enormous physical and mental agony he was subjected to. According to the law of the Han Dynasty, money could be used to exempt someone from the death penalty. Sima Qian had a low official rank and was too poor to pay to commute his sentence. However he knew that to complete *The Records of the Grand Historian*, he had to live. Hence, he confessed to the crime he was accused of and escaped the death penalty. However, he suffered castration which was a burning shame for him. But just in order to write his famous book, Sima Qian outlived this terrible time in his life. In 96 BC, Emperor Wu changed the tenor of his reign and implemented a general pardon. Sima Qian, now over 50 years old, was released from prison. He took the post of Prefect of the Palace Writers and began to write *The Records of the Grand Historian* attentively. In 91 BC, it was finally completed.

The book recorded Chinese history over 3,000 years from the time of the Yellow Emperor until the reign of Emperor Wu.

Sima Qian Writes 'The Records of the Grand Historian'

With over 500,000 Chinese characters, the book comprises 12 volumes of *Imperial Biographies*, 10 volumes of *Tables*, 8 volumes of *Treatises*, 30 volumes of *Biographies of the Feudal Houses and Eminent Persons* and 70 volumes of *Biographies and Collective Biographies*, totaling 130 volumes. In the book, the historical facts are reliable and the comments and remarks generally fair and even-handed. It is really a remarkable memoir.

The Records of the Grand Historian is the first general historical text written in the biographical style in the history of China. It is a great historical book and a prominent literary work and is one of the jewels of Chinese literary culture

Zhaojun Departs for the Frontier

Wang Zhaojun was born into a prominent family in what is now Xingshan County in Hubei Province during the reign of Emperor Yuan (48 BC-33 BC) of the Western Han Dynasty (206 BC-25 AD) . Zhaojun was a very beautiful girl, and when she was old enough, she was selected to enter the harem of Emperor Yuan.

These girls who entered the emperor's harem were like birds shut in a cage, as they lost all freedom. Living a lonely and monotonous life in the harem, these beautiful and lovely girls idled away their youth. It was more difficult for them to meet the emperor than to ascend to heaven, because when he chose a new wife, the Emperor was first presented with portraits of all the beautiful women in the land. Only those who caught his eyes could be selected to wait on him.

In order to gain the emperor's favor, many ladies-in-waiting bribed the imperial painter Huang Yanshou in order that he would flatter them in his painting.

Wang Zhaojun, who was very honest and straightforward, was not willing to pay a bribe, so Mao Yanshou did not paint her as beautiful as she really was. Though she had been in the harem for many years, she never seen the emperor.

In 33 BC, Huhanye visited Chang'an on a tribute trip, and he paid a formal visit to Emperor Yuan of the Han Dynasty. He took the opportunity to ask that he be allowed to become an imperial son-in-law.

In the past, the Han court often selected

a princess or a daughter born to the imperial family and married her to a Shanyu. This time, Emperor Yuan of the Han Dynasty decided to choose one of his concubines from the imperial harem for Shanyu. He gave orders, saying, "Whoever is willing to go to the Hun will be regarded as a princess by the Emperor."

Instead of honouring the Chanyu with a princess, Huhanye was presented with five women from the imperial harem, one of them who was Wang Zhaojun.

Almost all the ladies-in-waiting wished to leave the palace. However no one responded because nobody wanted to go to the distant and desolate Hun area.

Wang Zhaojun stood up and volunteered to join the Shanyu, which greatly pleased the minister who was sent to handle the affair.

Emperor Yuan of the Han Dynasty bade the minister to choose a propitious day on which Huhanye Shanyu and Wang Zhaojun could get married in Chang'an.

Zhaojun Departs for the Frontier

When Huhanye Shanyu and Wang Zhaojun went to thank the emperor for his kindness before departing, the emperor saw the stunningly beautiful and elegant Wang Zhaojun for the first time. Her beauty amazed the Emperor and made him reconsider his decision to send her to the Hun. But he had to keep his word, so he gave her up regretfully.

After seeing them off, Emperor Yuan

felt very angry. He was especially enraged at the Painter Mao Yanshou, thinking that it was his fault because he had failed to paint Wang Zhaojun in all her glory. Then the Emperor had Mao executed.

Wang Zhaojun, along with Huhanye Shanyu, departed Chang'an. Braving the cold wind, she rode a horse, and made light of travelling a thousand km to the Hun. Wang was honoured as Ninghu Yanzhi. When Huhanye died, Wang Zhaojun requested to be allowed to return to China. Emperor Cheng, however, ordered that she follow the Hun custom and become the wife of the next Shanyu, her stepson, born by her husband's first wife.

Wang Zhaojun spread the culture of the Han Dynasty to the Hun and gained the love and esteem of the Hun people. Once she persuaded Huhanye Shanyu not to declare war against China. After that, peace was maintained for over 60 years between China and the Hun.

Cai Lun
Makes Paper

Chinese script first appeared during the
Shang Dynasty in China about 3,500 years
ago. The script was engraved on tortoise shells
and ox bones. During the Spring and Autumn
(770 BC-476 BC) and Warring States period
(475 BC-221 BC) writings and inscriptions
were generally made on tablets of bamboo or
wood. At the same time they were written on
pieces of silk called chih by imperial families
and noblemen. These materials had a number
of disadvantages. A tablet of bamboo was too

small. To write a book required thousands of bamboo tablets, joined with rope. Obviously this was very heavy and inconvenient to both read and carry and store. Silk was too thin and was thus inconvenient to use. It was also costly and thus not good for common use.

During the period of the Western Han Dynasty (206 BC-25 AD) paper was made. However, the paper was coarse in texture and inconvenient to write on. Therefore, many people were engaged in trying to find ways to make cheap and light material for writing.

During the period of the Eastern Han Dynasty (25-220), a eunuch name Cai Lun (c. 61-121) put his mind to his past experience in making paper and found paper making materials everywhere. After a lot of trial and error, he finally succeeded in manufacturing a new type of paper - at one tough and tensile and cheap.

Cai Lun's paper was made by cutting

up the bark of trees, remnants of hemp, cloth rags, and fishing nets, mashing them together, and then boiling them to get rid of all foreign bodies. The paper pulp would then be spread on the mat to dry in the sun. The dried flakes were taken off and thus sheets of paper were made.

In 105, Cai Lun submitted his paper

making process to the emperor of the Han Dynasty and received praise for his achievement. Cai Lun's new paper making technique became the standard everywhere. A decade later, Cai Lun was created the "Marquis of Longting"and the paper he made was universally called "the paper of Marquis Cai."

Paper was invented in China. Although paper existed in China before Cai Lun, his achievements lay in improving the technique for making jute paper and overseeing the development and standardization of manufactured paper.

Though not the inventor of paper making, Cai Lun was a real innovator. He initiated the idea of making paper from the bark of trees, the remnants of hemp, cloth rags, and fishing nets.

Cai Lun made paper from plant fiber with simple equipment and familiar materials, and this was a great event in the history of human culture. Papermaking, gunpowder, printing and the compass are known as the four great ancient inventions of the Chinese people. They have played an important role in the development of Chinese science and culture and serve as among the greatest contribution made by ancient China to world civilization.

Liu Bei Pays Three Visits to Sleeping Dragon Ridge

In the late years of the Eastern Han Dynasty (25-220), a peasant revolt, led by Zhao Jiao, broke out. The rebels wrapped their heads with yellow scarves, thus being known as the "Yellow Scarf Army."

Liu Bei (161-223), a native of Zhuo County (present-day Zhuoxian in Hebei) participated in the suppression of the Yellow Scarf Army, and in the process he managed to gather a small armed force.

Over two decades after the peasant revolt had been put down, the state remained in chaos. The Han court had no effective power. Cao Cao took the emperor from Chang'an to Xuchang. He was only prime minister in name, but he was actually the most powerful figure at court. The warlord Sun Qun set up an independent regime in East Wu, basically disregarding the court. The ambitious, Liu Bei, a descendant of the Han household, was frustrated as he felt he needed some talented people to assist him in the great tasks ahead.

Someone recommended a very capable man to Liu Bei. This man was Zhuge Liang who was known as "Mr. Sleeping Dragon." Liu Bei was eager to meet him.

Liu Bei prepared some rich gifts, and set out, with his sworn brothers Guan Yu and Zhang Fei, for Zhuge Liang's dwelling place - the Sleeping Dragon Range in Longzhong (present-day Xiang Fan in Hubei or Nanyang in Henan).

He knocked at the rough door of the cottage and was told that Zhuge Liang had already left. They had to return in

Liu Bei Pays Three Visits to Sleeping Dragon Ridge

disappointment.

Some days after, Liu Bei and his brothers were told that Zhuge Liang had come back. They braved the snow again to go to visit him. But Zhuge Liang had invited a friend to go out and had not returned. Again they did not met him.

Time slipped away till spring was near. Then Liu Bei selected a propitious day for another visit to Zhuge Liang. Guan Yu said, "Brother, you have sought him twice; surely this is showing too much deference. I do not believe this man can be so great; he is avoiding you and does not dare to face you. Why do you so obstinately continue to seek him out?"

"I think you are mistaken too,"agreed Zhang Fei. "How can this villager be such a marvel of wisdom? You should not go again and, if he will not come to you, I will bring him with a hempen rope."

Liu Bei replied, "In the past, Duke Huan of Qi paid a visit to the home of a common person five times, before finally meeting him. The man we are visiting is a true person of virtue."

When the three stood again at the door, Zhuge Liang was asleep. Liu Bei and his two brothers waited at the door quietly until he woke up.

Liu Bei cordially asked Zhuge Liang for his analysis of the current situation in

China. After making some modest remarks, Zhuge Liang gave a shrewd analysis of the situation and made a telling contrast between the various parties of the time. He proposed a feasible strategic plan for Liu Bei: Jingzhou to be taken first as a base, and the Western Land of Rivers next for the foundation of an empire. By reforming domestic politics, and allying with Sun Quan, making peace with the foreigners to the south and making peace with the Rongs to the west, he pointed out how Liu Bei could consolidate his support and rally more people to his banner. Then when the time was right he showed how Liu Bei could march north against Cao Cao and take power.

Liu Bei invited Zhuge Liang to join his leadership. This proved to Zhuge Liang the sincerity of his desire. Zhuge Liang left Longzhong and joined Liu Bei. Thus began the glorious political career of Zhuge Liang.

Emperor Yang of the Sui Dynasty Initiates the Digging of the Grand Canal

Emperor Yang Guang (569-618) was the second emperor of China's Sui Dynasty (581-618). He had managed to usurp his brother Yang Yong as the crown prince. After his father died, he killed Yang Yong and ascended to the throne.

Emperor Yang was one of the most notoriously debauched emperors in Chinese history. As soon as he ascended the throne in 604, he set about doing two major things: re-designing Luoyang, which he designated as the eastern capital, and the digging of a grand cannal running from south to north.

In 605, he gave orders to conscript over one million people in Henan and Huaibei to dig a canal called the "Tongji Canal" connecting Luoyang with Shanyang (present-day Huai'an in Jiangsu Province) on the south bank of the Huaihe River. Then another 100,000 people in the Huainan region were conscripted to dredge the Hangou Canal from Shanyang to Jiangdu (present-day Huan'an to Yangzhou), which had been built during the Spring and Autumn Period. This made the water and land transportation between Luoyang and the south of the Yangtze River very convenient. Then the Emperor ordered the dredging of two canals: the Yongji Canal from the north bank of the Yellow River in Luoyang to Zhuojun (present-day Beijing), and the Jiangnan River from Jingkou (present-day Zhenjiang in Jiangsu) to Yuhang (present-day Hangzhou in Zhejiang). Finally the four canals were linked into a Grand Canal running from the south (Hangzhou) to the north

(Beijing) with a total length of 1,794 km.

When the canal was completed it linked the river systems of the Qiantang River, the Yangtze River, the Huai River, the Yellow River, the Weihe River and the Haihe River. It is historically known as the Beijing-Hangzhou Grand Cannal.

After the completion of the canal from Luoyang to Jiangdu, Emperor Yang sailed to Jiangdu along with 200,000 followers. The flotilla, consisting of 10,000 ships and stretched about 100 km from beginning to end, all on canal waters.

The dragon ship that Emperor Yang traveled in was a four-storied ship and it housed a palace with over 100 rooms. The whole ship was decorated with flower patterns carved in gold and jade.

On his trip, Emperor Yang ordered officials to build a road which could be used only by the Emperor on both banks of the canal. He also employed 80,000 laborers to tow the huge flotilla and local cavalrymen to escort the flotilla.

Every time the huge flotilla anchored somewhere, local people had to come to offer them the very best food. There was so much food that the leftovers were buried in a pit. However, the common people who offered the food had hardly enough to eat themselves.

Emperor Yang went for a cruise nearly every year, on his great canal and cared little for the welfare of the common people. During his 14-year reign, he spent some nine years cruising on the Grand Canal.

The great work of the Grand Canal was built with the blood and sweat and toil and the lives of thousands of people. The decline of the Sui Dynasty was directly linked to the debauchery of Emperor Yang.

Emperor Yang had the Grand Canal dug to strengthen his administration over the whole country and to facilitate the transportation of materials from the south of the Yangtze River to the north. Of course, the main aim was to satisfy his own dissipated desires. But, as the great water transportation works in ancient China, the Beijing-Hangzhou Grand Canal was of immensely important significance to the development of the economy and culture of North China, and greatly facilitated the unification of the country.

The Incident at Xuanwu Gate

In the later years of the Sui Dynasty (581-618), the country was in turmoil. Realizing that the Sui Empire was facing collapse, many officials rose in revolt and declared themselves as emperor. In 615, Li Yuan, an important Sui minister and his sons raised troops in Taiyuan and overthrew the rule of the Sui Dynasty ((581-618). In 618, Li Yuan founded the Tang Dynasty (618-907), becoming Emperor Gaozu of Tang.

After the founding of the Tang Dynasty, Li Jiancheng, as the oldest son, was created crown prince, Li Shimin, the second son, the Prince of Qin, and Li Yuanji, the fourth son, the Prince of Qi.

Among the three brothers, Li Shimin was the ablest. He assisted his father in defeating their most powerful rivals and unifying the country, so he enjoyed greater prestige. Crown Prince Li Jiancheng, fearful that Li Shimin would contend for the throne with him, allied with Li Yuanji to secretly marginalize Li Shimin and together they plotted their brother's assassination. Li Shimin was not willing to give up the land he had gained, so there was both open strife and a behind the scenes power struggle between the princes.

The two brothers - Li Jiancheng and Li Yuanji - won the day with the help of some of Emperor Gaozu's favorite concubines. They asked them to speak ill of Li Shimin in front of their emperor father. This method worked and Emperor Gaozu became suspicious of Li Shimin.

Li Jiancheng invited Li Shimin for a

drink. When Li Shimin had drunk for a whil, he felt a sharp pain in his stomach. He knew then that his wine had been poisoned. He immediately returned home, thus narrowly avoiding death.

Li Jiancheng and Li Yuanji secretly wrote a letter to try to sow division between Li Shimin and his favorite general Yuchi Jingde. However, the plot failed. Li Shimin's allies all were loyal and devoted to their master.

In 626, the Eastern Turks (a minority in ancient China) had been incorporated into Tang territory. Li Jiancheng and Li Yuanji believed that this offered a good opportunity to get rid of Li Shimin. They wanted to transfer his trusted followers and troops there using the pretext of war on the frontier.

Seeing the danger, Li Shimin decided to act first and he staged a coup, partly at the urging of his brother-in-law Zhangsun Wuji .

On the second day of the 7th lunar month, Emperor Gaozu summoned the three brothers to the court to make inquiry about Li

Jiancheng and Li Yuanji's accusations.

Li Shimin ordered Yuchi Jingde to ambush a group of troops at Xuanwu Gate - the north gate to the Imperial Palace in Xi'an.

When Li Jiancheng and Li Yuanji arrived at the Xuanwu Gate, they began to sense that something was wrong, and so they began to head back to Li Jiancheng's palace.

Li Shimin personally chased after them and yelled out, "Big brother!"

Li Yuanji drew his bow and fired arrows at Li Shimin, but failed to hit him. Li Shimin fired an arrow at Li Jiancheng, killing him instantly.

Yuchi Jingde then arrived with a group of cavalryman. He chased Li Yuanji down and killed him with an arrow.

Li Shimin's guards kept out the armed escort of the crown prince and Prince of the Qi. Meanwhile, Li Shimin sent Yuchi into the palace with his guards, and Yuchi advanced all the way into Emperor Gaozu's presence, forcing Emperor Gaozu to accept the coup.

Three days later, Emperor Gaozu made Li Shimin crown prince. Eight months later, he passed the throne to Li Shimin, who became Emperor Taizong.

Li Shimin was the second emperor of the Tang Dynasty of China - one of the greatest emperors in Chinee history - Taizong.

Songtsan Gampo and Princess Wencheng

During the reign (627-649) of Emperor Taizong, the Tang Dynasty became a great center of East Asian civilization. Various states in the Western Regions established diplomatic and trade relations with Tang Dynasty. Tubo to the southwest of the Tang lands also sent emissaries there.

Tubo in ancient China gained in power and prestige from the 7th to the 9th century.

After ascending the throne of Tsampo (king), Songtsan Gampo unified Tubo, and establish his capital in present-day Lhasa, and founded a unified Tubo Kingdom. The Tubo Kingdom actively sought to establish closer ties with the Tang Dynasty.

In 634, Songtsan Gampo sent an embassy to pay tribute to the Tang Emperor, requesting that a daughter of the Han imperial family be offered in marriage to him. The Tang Emperor sent a minister to Tubo in response.

In 638, Songtsan Gampo sent an envoy to Chang'an (present-day Xi'an) with priceless jewels for the Emperor, requesting again a union through marriage. But Emperor Taizong did not consent. Military conflict broke out in the border areas between the two states. Before long, Songtsan Gampo withdrew his troops and sent an envoy to Tang Dynasty to try to make peace.

In 640, Songtsan Gampo sent an envoy to Chang'an with another proposal, expressing Tubo's sincere desire to establish friendly relations with the Tang Dynasty. Emperor Taizong finally consented and decided to marry Princess Wencheng to Songtsan

Gampo.

Princess Wencheng, a niece of Emperor Taizong, was bright and beautiful, and very dutiful. She set out for Tubo in 641. Emperor Taizong gave her a rich and generous dowry. Apart from treasures and classical books, there were all kinds of cookbooks, medical writings, medical instruments and the seeds of all sorts of grains and vegetables. In addition, a number of craftsmen also followed the princess into Tibet.

The dream that Songtsan Gampo had many years ago had come true. He went over to Bohai (present-day Maduo County in Qinghai Province) with his retinue to await the arrival of Princess Wencheng. He also built the "Bohai Imperial Palace" on the banks of Zhaling Lake and Eling Lake not far away from the source of the Yellow River, in which their wedding ceremony was to be held.

After entering Tubo, Princess Wencheng introduced many aspects of Chinese culture and advanced technology into Tubo. Together with Songtsan Gampo, she made a concerted effort to promote the development of the Tibetan economy and culture. At that time, the Tibetan people had no writing and kept records by knotting ropes or drawing marks. Inspired by Princess Wencheng, Songtsan Gampo ordered the creation of 30 Tibetan

letters. The craftsmen who had followed Princess Wencheng into Tubo spread advanced Han techniques, thus making their own contribution to Tibetan agricultural development.

In 650, Songtsan Gampo passed away, but Princess Wencheng still stayed in Tubo.

Princess Wencheng who lived in Tubo

for 40 years was loved and esteemed by the Tibetan people. She made a great contribution to promoting the friendly relationship between the Han and Tibetan peoples and Tibetan economic and cultural development.

To this day, the Jokhang Monastery and the Potala Palace house statues of Songtsan Gampo and Princess Wencheng. Ballads sung in praise of Princess Wencheng about 1,300 years ago are still in circulation among the common Tibetan people today.

Empress Wu Zetian

Wu Zetian (624-705) is the only female ruler in the history of China. Her father Wu Shihuo was one of the founders of the Tang Dynasty (618-907). He served as the Minister of Works and was ennobled as the Duke of Ying.

In 637, the 14-year-old Wu Zetian was summoned to the imperial palace and became a concubine of the Tang Emperor Taizong. At that time, her father had been dead for two years.

Wu Zetian was beautiful, clever and

erudite, and was duly appointed as "Cairen (Talented, a kind of rank among the imperial consorts) after entering the palace. After Emperor Taizong died, she was sent to an imperial temple to become a nun. She thought she would spend the rest of her life in the temple. Unexpectedly, Emperor Gaozong Li Zhi went to the temple one day to meditate and pray and he met her. This coincidence caused a major transition in Wu Zetian's life.

To estrange Emperor Gaozong from his favorite concubine Xiao, the Empress encouraged Emperor Gaozong to bring Wu Zetian back to the palace. However, after Wu Zetian returned to the palace, she gradually gained the favor of Emperor Gaozong.

In 655, Wu Zetian was appointed as Empress. She persuaded Emperor Gaozong to get rid of the ministers who were against her and killed the former Empress and concubine Xiao.

Emperor Gaozong was suffering from serious illness then. He was very weak and had to ask Wu Zetian to handle state affairs in his place.

In 683, Emperor Gaozong died. Wu Zetian appointed her two sons as emperors in succession; they were Emperor Zhongzong Li Xian and Emperor Ruizong Li Dan. However, even being the power behind the two emperors couldn't satisfy her.

In 690, Wu Zetian acceded to the "request" of the whole country to become emperor herself. She called herself "Sacred and Divine Empress Regnant" and changed the title of the reigning dynasty into "Zhou".

After Wu Zetian became the Emperor, she made every effort to make the country prosperous, encouraging and awarding those engaged in agriculture and mulberry planting and developing the economy. The prosperity of the country was thus maintained. She

initiated the system of imperial examinations and examined second-degree scholars in person. She asked people to recommend themselves to be officials above the ninth rank. However she also appointed cruel officials and stirred up a large-scale prison revolt. Lots of imperial clansmen and courtiers were butchered.

In her old age, Wu Zetian increasingly placed her trust in crafty and fawning officials. Her dynasty became more and more corrupt.

In 705, Wu Zetian fell terminally ill. The Prime Minister seized the opportunity to acclaim Zhongzong as emperor and honored Wu Zetian as "Empress Regnant Zetian Dasheng". In the winter of the same year, Wu Zetian died of illness at the age of 82. Before her death, Wu Zetian stripped herself of her imperial title removed and returned the country to the Family Li.

Wu Zetian was interred in a joint burial

with Emperor Gaozong at the Qianling Mausoleum. She wrote no epitaph to sing the praises of her like the emperors before her but erected a stele without inscription, with a view to letting later generations judge her merits and sins.

Today, the stele still stands at the Qianling Mausoleum, about 50 km northwest of Xianyang, Shaanxi. The stele is 7.53 meters high and 2.1 meters wide and weighs over 100 tons.

The An-Shi Rebellion and the Mutiny at Mawei

During the 30 years of the Kaiyuan Period under the reign (712-756) of the Tang Emperor Xuanzong, the social economy was unprecedentedly prosperous. But in the late Kaiyuan Period, the Emperor Xuanzong seemed to become another person, beginning to neglect state affairs and indulge himself in luxury and debauchery. At the age of 61, he fell in love with Yang Yuhuan and appointed her as a high-ranked imperial concubine. Later, he became further distracted and wouldn't listen to the counsel of his virtuous officials. He dismissed the excellent Prime Minister Zhang Jiuling and depended on the treacherous official Li Linfu. He also gave great power to a cousin of Concubine Yang, Yang Guozhong.

Li Linfu made show of serving the emperor but was a law onto himself in private, creating lots of trouble for the country. After he died, Yang Guozhong succeeded him as prime minister. After assuming the reins of government, this idiot blackballed dissidents, embezzled money and took bribes, making the court increasingly corrupt. Society fell into chaos.

In the 11th lunar month of 755, the Northern Defending General An Lushan in collusion with his subordinate Shi Siming launched a rebellion under the pretext of killing Yang Guozhong. This was the famous "An-Shi Rebellion" in history.

An Lushan was originally a Turki, one of the ethnic minorities in the north. He tried to ingratiate himself with Emperor Xuanzong

in as many ways as possible, even calling himself the adopted son of Xuanzong's favorite Concubine Yang. The emperor never dreamed that he would be the one to launch a rebellion.

The army of An Lushan quickly approached Chang'an. In great panic the emperor fled with Concubine Yang, Yang Guozhong and his sons and grandsons to

Sichuan.

The refugees had a cold reception from local officials. Eventually they arrived at a post house called Mawei.

The officers and soldiers accompanying the emperor were tired and hungry and full of complaints. They thought the turmoil had been caused by Yang Guozhong, so they killed Yang and his son as well as the three elder sisters of Concubine Yang. Then, they surrounded the residence of the emperor and asked him to execute Concubine Yang.

The emperor couldn't bear to kill his favorite concubine, but to save his own life, he had to surrender the concubine and ask her to hang herself.

After they heard the concubine was dead, they gave up and stopped besieging the residence of the emperor.

The death of Concubine Yang affected the emperor greatly. Later, he decided to give up his throne to the crown prince. Then, the prince and Emperor Xuanzong departed the post house. Emperor Xuanzong went to Sichuan to avoid the turmoil and the prince went northward to salvage what he could from the remnants of the defeated army.

In 756, Prince Li Xiang succeeded to the throne and honored Emperor Xuanzong as Emperor father.

In 757, An Lushan was killed by his son An Qingxu in Luoyang.

In 759, Shi Siming killed An Qingxu. Two years later, Shi Siming was also beheaded by his son Shi Chaoyi.

In 763, Shi Chaoyi was at a dead end and committed suicide while being besieged by various crusading armies. Hence, the rebellion was suppressed.

The rebellion lasted seven years, and seriously shook the political stability of the Tang Dynasty, destroying the social and economic development of the dynasty. The rule of the Tang Dynasty began to decline from then on. The country began to be riven by warlordism, with individual warlords each dominating their own region.

Acclaimed Emperor When Hungover and Consolidating Power Using Wine

From 907 to 960, China entered the period of the Five Dynasties. During these 40 years, China experienced the Five Dynasties of the Later Liang (907-923), Later Tang (923-936), Later Jin (936-947), Later Han (947-950) and Later Zhou (951-960).

In 959, the emperor of the Later Zhou died of illness. His son, only seven years old, succeeded to the throne. The political situation of the country was extremely precarious. Lots of officials in the court believed the young emperor would never be able to shoulder such a great task as ruling at such a difficult time. Hence, some people began to hatch plots, in an attempt to support General Zhao Kuangyin who had a lot of military support and who dreamt of becoming emperor.

On the first day of the first lunar month in 960, Zhao Kuangyin led his armies out of the capital under the pretext that there was conflict in the north.

On the third day of the first lunar month, the army of Zhao quartered at the Chenqiao Post House about 10 km northeast of Kaifeng. That night, Zhao Kuangyin drank heavily. Early the next morning, when he was still hungover, his younger brother Zhao Kuangyi and adviser Zhao Pu fetched out a yellow robe symbolizing imperial power and wrapped him in it. Not allowing him to speak, they demanded that he seek to become emperor. This was the "mutiny at Chenqiao Post House" in history.

It was said that Zhao Kuangyin who was not completely recovered from his revelry declined the honor again and again, but he found it hard to contend with the compelling force of his supporters. He had to lead the army back to the capital and take the throne from the young emperor. He founded the Song Dynasty (960-1127). Zhao Kuangyin proved to be a kind emperor with a good head on his shoulders and was very courageous.

Within 6 months of becoming emperor, two governors with extensive civil and military affairs launched rebellions. Though the rebellions were suppressed, the emperor still felt unsure of his position. The emperor knew his history. He saw that the warlords dominated many regions and the dynasty was not stable. He asked for advice from his Prime Minister Zhao Pu. Zhao Pu suggested that the court centralize all military leadership.

In 961, Zhao Kuangyin invited a group of high-ranking generals to his palace for a drink. He sighed heavily and said, "It is so hard to be an emperor. I would be happier to be a governor of a province. I could sleep well

all night long then." The others asked him his reasons. Zhao replied, "Everyone desires the throne. Though you are not disloyal, someone will put the yellow robe on you. Perhaps you will not be able to help yourself at that time." The others were greatly surprised to hear these humble words and they all asked the emperor for guidance. Zhao Kuangyin said, "You'd better surrender your military leadership and act as local officers. You can purchase farmland and houses. Later, I will marry my daughters to your sons. There will be strong links between us. Wouldn't that be better?" The others enthusiastically agreed.

After the banquet, the generals returned to their own homes. The next morning, Zhao Kuangyin received the resignations of many ministers who all desired to go home due to old age and illness.

Zhao Luangyin didn't break his promise. When approving the resignations, he awarded them large amounts of properties and asked them to become local governors. Later, he also held banquets at which he took away military power from each local governor in succession. Thus, all localized military power was returned to the central government. This was the famous history of "neutralizing military threats with wine". This unique move solidified the rule of the Song Dynasty.

Li Yu Loses His Kingdom

After the fall of the Tang Dynasty in 907, Five dynasties - the Later Liang (907-923), Later Tang (923-936), Later Jin (936-947), Later Han (947-951) and Later Zhou (951-960) - quickly succeeded one another in the north, and ten independent states - Wu, Wuyue, Min, Chu, Southern Han, Former Shu, Later Shu, Jingnan, Southern Tang and Northern Han - were established, mainly in the south.

The Southern Tang, one of the Ten Kingdoms, was founded in 937. The capital was located in Jinling (present-day Nanjing in Jiangsu Province). The state was named Tang (history would refer to it as the Southern Tang). The Southern Tang was conquered in 975 by the Northern Song. It was ruled by three emperors and lasted a total of 39 years.

Li Yu (937-978), the last ruler of the Southern Tang ascended the throne in 961. He is historically known as Li Houzhu (literally meaning the last lord of the Southern Tang).

This fertile land was large and prosperous compared to the other Ten States of that period. However, the three generations of emperors were so mediocre that they wasted all their natural advantages.

Li Yu was a very peculiar monarch. He was idiotic in terms of politics, but an excellent ruler in terms of the arts. He was skilled in calligraphy, music, painting, and poetry, especially the *ci* form. He has been called the "first true master" of the *ci* form in the history of Chinese poetry.

After founding the Song Dynasty, Zhao

Kuangyin launched successive military expeditions against the neighboring kingdoms. Several small states were easily conquered, so Li Yu began to panic. His first plan was to pay large tribute to the Song court so as to maintain his power. Then he wrote a letter to the Song emperor, saying that he was willing to discard the title of "Southern Tang" and to term himself "lord of the regions south of the Yangtze River." However, his proposals did nothing to change Zhao Kuangyin's determination to unify all China under the Song banner.

In 974, Song Emperor Taizu Zhao Kuangyin sent 100,000 troops to attack the Southern Tang by water and land. Arriving at the banks of the Yangtze River, the Song Dynasty armies prepared to cross the river by building a floating bridge in order to attack Jinling. Hearing this news, Li Yu did not believe it, and continued drinking with his ministers.

The Song Dynasty armies crossed the

Yangtze River and quickly arrived at the gates of Jinling. At that time Li Yu was chanting sutras and praying with the monks and Taoist priests in the palace. On the second day, he went up to the gate tower to make his rounds. Immediately he saw the banners of the Song Dynasty armies all around his capital. He immediately sent a special envoy to the capital of the Song Dynasty to sue for peace.

The peace talk failed and the two armies fought. The Southern Tang army was annihalated. Before the Song army could conquer his capital, Li Yu piled up a lot of straw in the palace. He planned to set fire to it and take his own life, but in the end he couldn't go through with it. He was taken captive by the Song Dynasty armies. The Southern Tang state ceased to be.

Li Yu was marched off to the capital of the Song Dynasty and was made the Marquess of Wei Ming (literally, the Marquess of Disobeyed Edicts) by Song Emperor Taizu.

Li Yu became a prisoner. However, his

best-known poems were composed during the years after the Song formally ended his reign in 975. Li's works from this period dwell on his lament for his lost kingdom and the pleasure it had brought him.

Song Emperor Taizu Zhao Kuangyin passed away in 976. Li Yu was poisoned by the Song emperor Taizong Zhao Jiong (namely Zhao Kuangyi) in 977.

Yue Fei and the Yue Army

Yue Fei (1103-1142) was a famous Chinese patriot and military general who fought for the Southern Song Dynasty (1127-1279) against the Jurchen armies of the Jin Dynasty (1115-1234). Yue was born into a poor tenant peasant's family. From childhood he displayed a genius for military tactics and carefully studied all martial arts knowledge.

Yue joined the army at the age of 19 when the Jurchen had founded the Jin Dynasty in North China. They constantly made incursions into the territory of the Song

Dynasty. In the fighting against the Jurchen armies, Yue Fei was bold and decisive and quickly became well-known. He led the Yue Army to victory after victory and basically secured the survival of the Song Dynasty.

After 1127, the court of the Southern Song Dynasty which was basically run by a cabal of debauched libertines, was content to exercise sovereignty over regions south of the

Yangtze River. Yue Fei detested these men and felt great compassion for the people who suffered cruel oppression at the hands of the Jin army. His ambition was always to retake this lost territory. To mollify him, the Emperor proposed building him a grand residence. Yue Fei declined, saying, "Our enemies have not been defeated, so I have no time to set up a home yet." When someone once asked this virtuous man to define "peace", Yue Fei said. "When civil officials do not have an itchy palm and military generals are not afraid to die, the world may know peace. "

Yue Fei imposed strict military discipline. Soldiers were not allowed to take people's straw without authorization. Anyone who violated army discipline would be punished severely. When the Yue Army passed by farms, no one dared to occupy the farmpeople's houses. They said, "Even if we freeze to death, we cannot break into people's houses and even if we starve to death, we cannot loot."

Yue Fei was famous for his care for his soldiers. He often personally prepared medicine for sick and injured soldiers. He also redistributed all properties that the court granted to him among his generals and soldiers.

When Yue armies fought, the generals would always be at the frontlines, and most often such an army was undefeatable. The Jin soldiers who fought the Yue Army coined the phrase, "It is easy to conquer a mountain, but difficult to conquer Yue Army."

In 1140, the Jin army attacked the Southern Song Dynasty. Yue Fei led his Army in a general counterattack against the Jin, and finally defeated the Jin army in Yancheng. The Yue Army marched forward triumphantly, gaining a great victory at Zhuxian Town, and began to make preparations to recover all of North China from the Jin.

Just when he was about to attack and retake Kaifeng, corrupt officials advised Emperor Gaozong to recall Yue Fei to the capital and sue for peace with the Jurchen. Fearing that a defeat at Kaifeng might cause the Jurchen to release arival for the Song throne, Qinzong, thus threatening his claim to the throne, the emperor followed their advice. The emperor and traitorous minister Qin Hui issued the "Twelfth Golden Edict" to Yue Fei, calling him back to the capital.

Yue Fei had to cease the attack and retreat so that the Southern Dynasty lost a golden opportunity to defeat the Jin army.

In 1142, Yue Fei was executed by Emperor Zhao Gou and Qin Hui on trumped-up charges. His son Yue Yun and general Zhang Xian were also killed.

The execution of Yue Fei was one of the great crimes of Chinese history.

Zhu Yuanzhang, an Emperor from Humble Origin

In the later years of the Yuan Dynasty (1271-1368), the court became practically paralyzed by internal factions fighting for control. The people suffered cruel oppression. During the reign of Emperor Shundi (1333-1341), the last emperor of the Yuan Dynasty, rebellion broke out all over the country.

Peasants led by Liu Futong rose in rebellion in 1351. They tied red scarves on their heads, and thus were referred to as the Red Turban Army. In the same year, Guo

Zixing also led a peasant revolt, and they were also called Red Turban Army.

In 1352, Zhu Yuanzhang (1328-1398) joined Guo Zixing's Red Turban Army. Because he was very brave and shrewd, he was quickly noticed by Guo Zixing, who married his adopted daughter Ma Xiuying to Zhu.

Zhu Yuanzhang became the well-known founder and first emperor (1368–1398) of the Ming Dynasty (1368-1644) of China.

Zhu Yuanzhang's birth name was Chongba. He was given the name Xingzong, and later Yuanzhang. Zhu was born into a poverty-stricken family, who lived by tilling leased farm land. At the age of 14 (in the spring of 1344) plague broke out in the Huaihe River valley, killing his father, mother and elder brother one after another. In order to survive, Yuanzhang became a monk in a monastery.

After joining the army at the age of 25, Zhu returned to his hometown to recruit followers, soon becoming Guo Zixing's right

hand man. After Guo died of illness, Zhu began to lead the army.

Zhu's military force got strong gradually. Zhu was able to attract many talented followers. He gained the upper hand on the troublesome warlords - the source of great strife in the later years of the Yuan Dynasty. Zhu's forces defeated all the major warlords.

In 1368 Zhu proclaimed himself the

Ming emperor, established his capital in Jingdu (present-day Nanjing in Jiangsu Province) and adopted "Hongwu" as the title of his reign. In the same year, he conquered Dadu (present-day Beijing), and formally ended the rule of the Yuan Dynasty. China became once again unified under the Ming.

Zhu Yuanzhang, as a civilian emperor, was very capable and decisive. He was a fierce and powerful personality. Having come from a peasant family, he knew only too well how much the peasants suffered from the exactions of the gentry and the wealthy. At the very beginning of his rule, he ordered that a census be carried out. He measured all land, promoted good farming practice and sericulture, equalized tax rates and corvee labor rules, constructed irrigation systems and dikes, opened up wasteland and relaxed restrictions on craftsmen. To control tyrannical and corrupt officials, he formulated the Code of the Great Ming. He also abolished the post of prime minister in order to concentrate absolute authority in his own hands,

Through a series of reform in politics and military affairs, the society of the Ming Dynasty in early days enjoyed harmony and stability. As time went by, Emperor Hongwu increasingly feared rebellions and coups. He conducted a violent purge of his enemies, real and perceived, which lasted some ten years in order to secure the power of his family. Most of the ministers who were with him when he founded the dynasty were killed at this time.

Hu Weiyong was among them. He and his family were killed because he was accused of attempting to usurp the throne. He Shanchang had two Iron Dan book coupons which should have exempted him from punishment, but he and his family, over 70 people in all, were killed when he was over 70 years old.

Song Lian who was honored as "master" by Zhu Yuanzhang lived discretely all his life, but he died on his way to a distant place to serve penal servitude after being prosecuted by the paranoid emperor.

The emperor of humble origins became one of the most infamous emperors for atrocities and autocracy in Chinese history.

Zheng He's Voyages

When speaking of Zheng He's voyages, there is a story commonly told among Chinese people. After Emperor Taizu died, the throne was passed to Zhu Yunwen (Ming Emperor Huidi), the grandson of Emperor Taizu. This greatly angered and disappointed the son of Emperor Taizu, the Prince of Yan, Zhu Di. Zhu Di sent troops southward from Beijing to attack the Capital Yingtian (present-day Nanjing). He took the throne from his nephew and made himself emperor. He became Emperor Chengzu. However, Emperor Huidi disappeared in the turmoil. Zhu Di was worried about this - worried that Emperor Huidi was hiding among the common people or might even have escaped abroad. Hence, he decided to send a fleet abroad to search for the missing Emperor. This is how Zheng He came to make his voyages. Of course, the true reason for Zheng He's voyages was not finding Emperor Huidi at all. It is just an interesting folk legend.

China was strong and prosperous during the Yongle Period (1403-1424) of the Ming Dynasty (1368-1644). Emperor Chengzu Zhu Di sent the eunuch Zheng He (1371-1433) to lead a fleet to explore the oceans to the west of the South China Sea and the islands and lands there. The purpose of Zheng He's voyages was to develop economic and cultural exchanges and to expand the influence of the Ming Dynasty.

In 1405, the fleet, commanded by 34-year-old Zheng He, set out from Liujiagang in Taicang in Jiangsu Province. It was the first of

his great voyages.

Zheng He was born in what is now Yunnan Province, and was named Ma Sanbao. Both his grandfather and father were Muslims and had even made the pilgrimage to Mecca. Zheng He became a eunuch in the palace of the Prince of Yan and gradually gained the prince's trust. The name Zheng He was given

to him by Emperor Chengzu.

On his first voyage, Zheng He's fleet of 62 ships carried well over 27,000 men, including sailors, soldiers, technical personnel, interpreters, doctors, etc., and large amounts of gold, precious stones, porcelain and silk. The largest ship had four layers of decks and was about 145 meters long, which was amazing for that time.

Whenever he landed in a new territory,

Zheng He first handed over a letter from the Chinese Emperor to the king of that state and presented gifts to him to show their friendship. Many states, seeing the size of the fleet and the lack of hostility, received them with open arms.

On his first voyage, Zheng He reached among many other places Champa (in present-day south Vietnam), Java (present-day Indonesia), Polembang (present-day southeast Sumatra), Malacca, Calicut and Ceylon. In September of the third year of the voyage, the fleet returned to China, with envoys sent by the kings of the states which Zheng He had visited.

From 1405 to 1433, Zheng He made seven voyages in all, visiting over ten countries along the Indian Ocean. The voyages even took Zheng He to the eastern coast of Africa.

In 1433, on the way back on his last voyage, Zheng He died of illness in Calicut on the western bank of the Indian Ocean and was buried there.

Nurhaci Founds the Later Jin Dynasty

The Jurchen were an ancient ethnic minority in China, originating from Heishui Mohe of the Tang Dynasty (618-907). In the late Northern Song Dynasty (960-1127), Wanyan Aguda unified the Jurchen tribes and founded the Jin Dynasty (1115-1234). In the middle period of the Ming Dynasty (1368-1644), the Jurchens began to merge with the local Han people and the area where they lived began to move southwards. In the Ming Dynasty, the Jurchens were divided into Jianzhou Jurchens, Haixi Jurchens and

Wild Jurchens. The Central Government of the Ming Dynasty established administrative bodies in the Jurchen areas to manage military and political affairs.

In the middle years of the Ming Dynasty, the three major Jurchen tribes in the Changbaishan Mountains and Heilongjiang River attacked each other and within each tribe, there were also internecine disputes.

Nurhaci (1559-1626), surnamed Aisin Gioro, was born in Hetuala (present-day Xinbin in Liaoning). Both his grandfather and father were junior chieftains of the Zuowei Clan of Jianzhou Jurchens and were appointed officials of the Ming Dynasty.

In 1583, the chieftain of the Jianzhou Jurchens Atai launched a rebellion. Nikan Wailan, the head of Tulun Town under the Suksuhu River tribe led the Ming troops to suppress the rebellion. In the course of suppressing the rebellion, the Ming troops slaughtered the father and grandfather of Nurhaci by mistake. At that time, Nurhaci, who was the Commander of Zuowei in Jianzhou, petitioned the Ming court that Nikan Wailan be handed over for punishment. However, his request was rejected. Nurhaci swore to unleash his troops decked out in the suits of armor left by his father to seek vengeance against his sworn foe Nikan Wailn.

Nurhaci occupied the Tulun Town of Nikan Wailan and drove him away. He also took the chance to attack other tribes of Jianzhou Jurchens. Within five or six years, Nurhaci had conquered all the other tribes of Jianzhou Jurchens and had killed Nikan Wailan. In 1593, Nurhaci united the Jianzhou Jurchens.

Subsequently, the ambitious Nurhaci began to launch wars to unify other Jurchen tribes. To preclude interference from the Ming Dynasty, he built up his forces in secret and at the same time pledged allegiance to the Ming emperor. In 1595, Nurhaci was made Dragon

and Tiger General.

Over 30 years, Nurhaci conquered all the major tribes of Haixi Jurchens and Wild Jurchens through force of arms.

In 1616, Nurhaci declared himself Khan and founded the Jin Dynasty, taking the Chinese imperial title, Tianming and making Hetuala his capital. In the 12th and 13th centuries, Wanyan Aguda of the Jurchens had founded a Jin Dynasty (1115-1234), so the Jin Dynasty founded by Nurhaci is known as the Later Jin to differentiate between the two dynasties.

In 1618, Nurhaci rose in rebellion against the Ming Dynasty. In the Battle of Saerhu, Nurhaci smashed the main force of the Ming army outside the Shanhaiguan Pass. Nurhaci moved his capital to Liaoyang in 1621 and to Shenyang in 1625.

In 1626, Nurhaci attacked the Ming troops in Ningyuan City (present-day

Xingcheng in Liaoning), but was defeated by the defending general Yuan Chonghuan. He was seriously wounded and died soon after.

In 1636, the successor of Nurhaci Hong Taiji declared himself emperor, changing the title of the dynasty from "Jin" to "Qing".

After the Qing Dynasty (1644-1911) was founded, Nurhaci was conferred with the posthumous title Taizu.

Zheng Chenggong Reoccupies Taiwan

In 1645, namely the second year after the downfall of the Ming Dynasty (1368-1644), the Prince of Tang Zhu Yujian, an imperial clansman of the Ming Dynasty declared himself emperor with the support of General Zheng Zhilong who had overseen the defence of Fujian and established the Longwu regime of the Southern Ming to resist the Qing Dynasty (1644-1911). In the following year, the Qing army went southward and Zheng Zhilong changed sides and pledged allegiance to the Qing Dynasty, but his 23-year-old son

Zheng Chenggong (1624-1662), a young general, was unwilling to surrender. He urged his father not to surrender but to no avail. Then, he fled to Nan'ao Island to try to recruit a military force to begin again the fight against the Qing army. In the following 10-odd years, with the support of the ordinary people, Zheng Chenggong managed to establish a large-scale navy and he gradually became the main force opposing the Qing in the southeastern coastal areas. At the height of his power, Zheng Chenggong had 72 batallions of land forces and 20 of naval force, totaling some 200,000 soldiers with over 5,000 ships. His army completely controlled the sea areas south of the Yangtze River Estuary and north of Tonkin Bay.

In 1661, it was clear that the Qing Dynasty had succeeded in unifying all of China. Zheng Chenggong faced an increasingly difficult situation. He weighed up the pros and cons and again and decided to move his army to Taiwan and drive away the foreign invaders who occupied the island. He hoped to make Taiwan his base for attacking the Qing court and restoring Ming power.

Taiwan has been part of the territory of China since ancient times. In the late Ming Dynasty, Dutch explorers and adventurers had taken advantage of the weaknesses of the Ming Dynasty to forcibly occupy Taiwan. They built castles, and levied exorbitant taxes on the people of Taiwan. The people of Taiwan were in a constant state of revolt but these rebellions were suppressed by the Dutch invaders.

On April 21, 1661, Zheng Chenggong set out with his army from Jinmen with over 400 ships. Despite the stormy waters, they crossed the Taiwan Straits and arrived at the Pescadores Islands. On the Pescadores Islands, Zheng Chenggong let his troops rest for several days and then he organized a great oath-taking ceremony. All the officers and soldiers of his army swore that they would reoccupy Taiwan.

Six days later, a great banner emblazoned with the characters "Zhaotao Grand General of the Great Ming" was erected on the lead ship. Zheng Chenggong led the army onto Taiwan Island at Luermen.

The Dutch invaders fell into a great panic. They gathered their soldiers at two castles called Taiwan (in the present day Dongping area of Taiwan) and Chihkan (present day Tainan) to confront the army of Zheng Chenggong.

Zheng Chenggong laid siege to Chihkan Castle and inflicted many defeats on the invaders. The invaders cowered in the castle and wouldn't come out. Zheng ordered that the castle's supply of water be cut off. Several days later, the Dutch solders surrendered.

Subsequently, Zheng Chenggong led the army to Taiwan Castle. Avoiding the invaders advantages - invulnerable castle and powerful cannon - Zheng Chenggong deployed his troops to reoccupy all other places on the Taiwan Island. Eight months later, Zheng Chenggong ordered the shelling of Utrecht Castle, an important beachhead just outside Taiwan Castle. This was the beginning of his final attack on Taiwan Castle. Losing hope of reinforcements, the Dutch invaders had no option but to raise the white flag and surrender.

On February 1, 1662, the Dutch general came to the Zheng Chenggong to officially surrender. Soon after all Dutch troops left Taiwan.

However not long after his great triumph, Zheng Chenggong died of illness.

Zheng Chenggong had retaken reoccupied Taiwan from foreign invaders, and thus he is rightly regarded as an outstanding national hero in the history of China.

Cao Xueqin and 'A Dream of the Red Mansions'

A Dream of the Red Mansions, which is sometimes also called *The Story of the Stone,* was written in the mid-17th century. The novel is generally acknowledged to be among the very best of classical Chinese novels. Over the past three centuries years, it has exerted a profound influence on the cultural life of the Chinese people.

The novel tells the story of four noble families - the Jia, Shi, Wang and Xue. In particular the novel depicts the rise to prosperity and the subsequent fall of the Ning and Rong Houses of the Jia clan. *A Dream of the Red Mansions* is essentially a love story as it tells the story of the tragic fate suffered by characters like Jia Baoyu and a group of girls in the Red Mansions under the feudal system. Its main protagonists Jia Baoyu and Lin Daiyu are a pair of youths madly in love and rebelling against the dishonesty of noblemen and the inherent unfairness of the feudal ethical code. Their love is doomed to end in tragedy. Lin Daiyu dies alone of illness while Jia Baoyu runs away because he is deceived into marrying a girl he has no love for. Despite previously enjoying high status and great wealth, their aristocratic family, collapses into penury and obscurity.

The novel also describes the dissolute and debauched lives of many Chinese feudal noblemen at that time; it exposes the oppression and exploitation of the working classes; it celebrates the young people, the servants and maids and the ordinary people who rebel against this restrictive and oppressive system. The novel castigates many aspects of traditional thought such as the feudal ethical code. Epic in scale this book is a stunning artistic, cultural and social achievement.

Cao Xueqin (1715-1763 or 1724-1764), the author of *A Dream of the Red Mansions*, was born of noble origin. Since the time of Cao Xueqin's great-grandfather, the Cao clan held the office of Imperial Textile Commissioner at Jiangning. They were in charge of purchasing textiles and clothes for the imperial family. Indeed, Cao Xueqin's grandfather, Cao Yin, when he was a child was a playmate of the young Emperor Kangxi (who would reign as Emperor from 1662 to 1732). So the Cao clan was a rich and powerful family.

The family's fortunes remained

prosperous until Kangxi's death and the ascension of Emperor Yongzheng to the throne. Internal strife in the imperial family meant that the Cao clan who lost favor with Emperor Yongzheng. The Emperor dismissed the Cao Xueqin's father from his post and confiscated all the Cao clan's properties. Cao Xueqin, still a young child at that time, shared in his family's misfortune.

The Cao family fell into penury. They were forced to relocate to Beijing and their lives became more and more difficult. His father passed away and Cao eventually found himself living in the western suburbs of Beijing. Sometimes, the whole family had nothing to eat but thin gruel.

Thus Cao Xueqin was intimately acquainted with a life of poverty and want and he came to know well a whole range of ordinaru working poor people. When he thought about the old days when his family

enjoyed high status and great prosperity, he sighed deeply with heartfelt emotion. Cao Xueqin had a very good knowledge of the vicissitudes of life when he came to begin writing his great novel *A Dream of the Red Mansions*.

Cao Xueqin spent a decade writing the first 80 chapters of the novel. However, the novel remained unfinished when the author, worn down by years of poverty passed away. After Cao's death, the novel circulated in a rough manuscript. It grew in popularity and many people after reading the first 80 chapters, craved an ending to the novel. They were so eager to find out what became of such fascinating characters. Some years later a writer named Gao E wrote an additional 40 chapters and his contribution became generally accepted as the conclusion to the great novel.

A Dream of the Red Mansions is well-known as a veritable encyclopaedia of Chinese feudal society. Over the past 200-plus years, people have read this book again and again and it has provoked tears, laughter and heated discussion. Many scholars have made careers out of analyzing this masterpiece of literature. 'Redology' - the study of A Dream *of the Red Mansions* is now effectively an independent field in the area of Chinese social science study and it focuses exclusively on this work.

Humen Opium Destruction

In the mid-Qing Dynasty, China's power and prestige declined dramatically. Western capitalist countries, led by Great Britain, driven by the Industrial Revolution and their increasingly advanced military and naval power, became the dominant powers in the world. They wanted more than anything to open up foreign markets in order to find extra markets for the vast quantities of goods manufactured in their great factories. They cast covetous eyes on the enormous Chinese market.

What the British Empire wanted to trade for the goods they coveted in China was not a common commodity. It was opium - a powerfully addictive and destructive force wherever it took hold in the world. Merchants from the British Empire tried every underhand trick they could think of to try to open Qing China to opium.

Opium from the British Empire flooded into China and vast quantities of silver poured out of China into the pockets of rich British Empire merchants. Before long more than two million Chinese were hopelessly addicted to opium and led lives of unbelievable misery.

Many people realized that opium constituted a poisonous threat to the harmony of Chinese society. There was a lot of popular support for a ban on opium despite the flourishing trade. Lin Zexu, then Governor-General of Hunan and Guangdong, submitted a memorial to the Emperor in 1838, in which he pointed out that if opium-smoking and the opium trade were not banned, China would before long have no effective troops to defend the country.

Lin Zexu was sent to Guangdong as imperial commissioner by the Daoguang Emperor (who reigned from 1821-1850) in December 1838 to halt the importation of opium by the British.

Lin Zexu (1785-1850) was a native of Fujian province. Because of his integrity and his outstanding achievements in his post, he was greatly loved and esteemed by the common people.

Upon arriving in Guangzhou in March 1839, he immediately put up a notice, ordering that all local opium traders surrender all their opium to the Chinese authorities and sign a 'no opium trade' bond, the breaking of which would be punishable by death.

On March 24, Lin ordered the suspension of trade between China and Britain and dispatched troops to surround the British Chamber of Commerce. The British Chief Superintendent of Trade in China, Charles

Elliot, got the British traders to agree to hand over their opium stock, which weighed a total of 1.15 million kg.

Lin had two pools, each about 40meters long and 50 meters deep dug on the beach in Humen, Guangdong. These pools were used to destroy the opium.

On June 3, 1839, Lin and his supporters supervised the destruction of the impounded opium. Chests of opium were pounded to pieces and cast into the pools. The opium was soaked in the water drawn from the Pearl River, and sea salt and lime were added to it. The lime, on coming in contact with the water, immediately began to bubble and boil. The opium was completely destroyed.

The destruction of the vast quantity of opium lasted 23 days.

In order to put an end to opium smuggling, Lin decreed that any ship found smuggling opium would be confiscated and the traders would be sentenced to death.

Lin Zexu's Opium Destruction in Humen showed the world China's determination to fight back against foreign domination.

Burning of the Old Summer Palace

In 1856, British and French imperialists provoked a series of incidents in China and the Second Opium War broke out.

With support from the United States and Russia, the coalition used their overwhelming naval power to briefly capture the Taku Forts near Tianjin in May, 1858. In June 1858, the corrupt and inept Qing court signed the Treaties of Tianjin with Britain, France, Russia, and the United States, humiliating the nation and effectively forfeiting any notion of independent Chinese sovereignty.

Britain and France were not satisfied with these massive concessions, and they planned to expand their war against China using the pretext of going to Beijing to exchange treaties.

In July 1860, a large Anglo-French force, numbering some 25,000 troops, landed near Beitang, and captured Dagu and Tianjin. On September 21, they defeated the Qing troops, who in truth offered little effective resistance, at Baliqiao in Tongzhou (present-day Beijing) before proceeding toward Beijing.

On September 22, Emperor Xianfeng (who reigned from 1851 to 1861) fled the capital for his Summer Resort in Jehol (present-day Chengde in Hebei Province), leaving his brother, Prince Gong in charge of negotiations.

Hearing a rumor that the Qing emperor had fled to the Old Summer Palace, Anglo-French troops marched there via Anding Gate and Desheng Gate.

The Old Summer Palace, one of the

great architectural wonders of the world, was first constructed during the Ming Dynasty (1368-1644). It was located in the northwestern suburbs of Beijing, began in the Ming Dynasty. In 1709, the Qing Emperor Kangxi granted it to his fourth son (later Emperor Yongzheng) as a gift and gave it the name "Garden of Perfect Brightness". After over 150 years of renovation and expansion, it was an amazingly ornate construction with picturesque scenery and uncountable treasures. Featuring gardens modeled after those common in the regions south of the Yangtze River, and also some western garden architecture styles, it was known as one of the most beautiful palace and grounds in all the world. All kinds of priceless treasures, unique historical books and records and precious historical cultural relics were kept there, making it also one of the largest museums in the world.

The Anglo-French troops faced only token resistance from a few Qing troops in the north of Beijing. On October 6, the Qing troops fled and at dusk, some French troops broke through the main gate of the Old Summer Palace, where they encountered much tougher resistance from a few score eunuches most of whom were killed in the fighting. At seven o' clock, they occupied the Old Summer Palace. Wenhai, the minister in charge of the Palace, could not bear the shame and he took his own life by throwing himself into the river in the Summer Palace and drowning himself.

On the second day, the British troops also marched into the Old Summer Palace. They soon began crazily looting all the great treasures.

There were so many rare treasures so that no one really knows even today how many were destroyed. The Anglo-French troops crowded into the Old Summer Palace in all directions. They looted whatever they saw and smashed whatever they could not take away. By October 9, when the invaders withdrew temporarily, the Old Summer Palace was absolutely devastated.

After it had been plundered, the British set fire to the Palace on October 18 and 19 to cover up their crimes and frighten the Qing court into further submission. The fire blazed for a full three days. The smoke hung over the sky above the city of Beijing and did not disperse for a long time. The fire also killed over 300 eunuches, maids-in-waiting and carpenters who refused to leave the Palace. Emperor Xianfeng who had fled to Jehol signed the Treaty of Beijing with Britain and France,. These unequal treaties pretty much turned China into a quasi-colony and the Chinese people faced more years of suffering and hardship.

The outrage committed by the British and French troops is astounding, and even today it enrages patriotic Chinese sensibilities. The destruction of the Gardens of Perfect Brightness is still regarded in China as a symbol of foreign aggression and humiliation.

Zuo Zongtang Recovers Xinjiang

Xinjiang is located in the northwest of China. As early as the Han Dynasty (206 BC-220 AD), the central government began to establish an administrative system in these far western regions. During the Yuan (1271-1368), Ming (1368-1644) and Qing (1644-1911) Dynasties, the central government implemented effective management over the regions. In the 1860s, the people of various ethnic groups in Xinjiang, influenced by Muslim uprisings in northwest China, rebelled against the rule of the Qing Dynasty. Xinjiang was rocked by successive waves of rebellion. Some even colluded with the forces of Tsarist Russia, with a view to separating from China completely.

At that time, Xinjiang was carved up into a number of separate regimes each ruled by rival warlords. Jin Xiangyin, the feudal lord of Kashgar in south Xinjiang, threw his lot in with the Khanate of Kokand. In 1865, the Khanate of Kokand sent Yaqub Beg to invade Xinjiang and occupy Kashgar. Two years later, Yaqub Beg brazenly declared the establishment of the "Khanate of Yatta Shahar" (meaning seven cities) and claimed himself Khan. In 1870, Yaqub Beg controlled all of the south of Xinjiang and part of the north of Xinjiang. In the meantime, Tsarist Russia also invaded and occupied Ili, making the situation in Xinjiang even more precarious.

With regard to the crisis in Xinjiang, there was dissension in the Qing court. Some officials wanted to focus on coastal defence and some wanted to focus on frontier defence. Those in favor of coastal defence suggested abandoning northwest Xinjiang and stressed how vital it was to protect southeast Xinjiang. But those who wanted to focus on frontier defence were fearful that the Russians wanted to swallow up Xinjiang and that they needed to be confronted. The Governor-General of Shaanxi and Gansu Zuo Zongtang (1812-1885) said, "Xinjiang is the doorway to China. If it is abandoned, there will be trouble for Gansu and Shaanxi and Shanxi and Inner Mongolia will inevitably become embroiled. Even Beijing will not be safe."

In 1875, the sickly Zuo Zongtang, who was over 60 years old, was appointed as the minister in charge of Military affairs in Xinjiang.

In 1876, Zuo led an army divided into three parts into Xinjiang via three separate routes. His strategy was to occupy the north of Xinjiang first and then advance slowly while winning quickfire battles. The army of

Zuo Zongtang first reoccupied Urumqi and its surrounding areas and then attacked Turpan. In 1877, Yaqub Beg was defeated at Korla by the Uygur people and the Qing army; he was shot down by his subordinate. The Qing army thus reoccupied Kashgar. In 1878, except for Ili, all of Xinjiang was back under Chinese control.

At the beginning of 1880, the Qing government sent Zeng Jize to Russia to

negotiate about the issue of Ili. To strengthen Zeng Jize's position for his diplomatic mission, Zuo Zongtang marched his army to Hami and established an anti-Russian headquarters at Hami. On the way to Hami, Zuo Zongtang ordered his soldiers to carry a coffin before them, a clear signal that they were not afraid to die in the fight against Russia in order to retake Ili.

Zuo Zongtang had no regard for his own safety. His support for Zeng Jize's diplomatic mission finally compelled Russia to return Ili to China.

Since the Opium War (1840-1842), Zuo Zongtang was undoubtedly the person who made the largest contribution to the Chinese nation.

Reform Movement of 1898

The Reform Movement of 1898 was a political reform movement of bourgeois reformists.

In April 1895, the Qing government was defeated in the Sino-Japanese War of 1894-1895 and was compelled to sign the Treaty of Shimonoseki with Japan - a severe humiliation for China. When the news spread to Beijing, public anger ran very high. Kang Youwei and others who were participating in the general examinations in Beijing mobilized over 1,300 successful candidates

in the imperial examinations from various provinces to submit a written statement to Emperor Guangxu opposing the signing of the Treaty of Shimonoseki. They advocated political reform and organized the Society for National Renewal, thus launching the reform movement. Kang Youwei, Liang Qichao and others organized societies for national renewal in various cities to advocate reform, and the movement soon spread throughout the country. The political force of the bourgeois reformists led by Kang Youwei gained the support of many important officials.

In the winter of 1898, Germany forcibly occupied Kiaochow Bay. The imperialist conspiracy to carve up China was finally revealed. Kang Youwei hurried to Beijing to present a memorial demanding that the emperor carry out reforms.

In April 1898, Kang Youwei and others, with the aim of protecting the country, the Chinese nation and the education system, advocated the establishment of a Society for the Study of Self-Renewal in Beijing.

On June 11, 1898, Emperor Guangxu issued an edict, declaring the implementation of reforms. He appointed Kang Youwei as an official in the Ministry of Foreign Affairs to take charge of carrying out reforms. During this period, Emperor Guangxu issued a series of edicts and decrees on reforms, concerning the study of culture, scientific technology and the managerial systems of western countries, developing capitalism and establishing a constitutional monarchy.

At that time, the real power of the Qing government was held by the Empress Dowager Cixi. The implementation of reform threatened her power, so she was determined to overthrow Emperor Guangxu. Kang Youwei and the other reformists began to hedge their bets and sought support from Yuan Shikai, a very powerful minister. Yuan Shikai agreed but spoke out of turn on the issue to Ronglu, a favorite of Empress Dowager Cixi. Inevitably the Empress Dowager found out.

Late in the night of September 21, 1898, the Empress Dowager Cixi launched her coup. She had Emperor Guangxu imprisoned and issued a decree to declare that she now held power. Subsequently, she ordered that the most prominent reformists be arrested and killed.

Kang Youwei had already left Beijing and Liang Qichao had escaped to the Japanese

Consulate. Dozens of reformists were arrested.
Of these, Tan Sitong, Yang Rui, Lin Xu, Liu
Guangdi, Yang Shenxiu and Kang Guangren
were beheaded at Caishikou in Beijing on
September 28. Tan Sitong remained calm
before his execution. Defiantly he cried with
his last breath "I go to my death happily in
the knowledge that what I fought for was the

good of China!"

Subsequently, Empress Dowager Cixi dismissed from office a large number of officials who had supported reform and abolished all reform decrees issued by Emperor Guangxu.

The Reform Movement of 1898 thus ended in failure.

The Reform Movement of 1898 was a progressive movement with far-reaching influence. Its failure proved that the road of bourgeois reform was a blind alley in China.

The Revolution of 1911

The Revolution of 1911 was a Chinese bourgeois democratic revolution which broke out on October 10, 1911.

Just before the revolution, the decadent Qing Dynasty was in terminal decline and had become basically a flunky of the imperialist powers. There was a large degree of social chaos in China at this time. A number of resistance movements launched popular rebellions. The bourgeois revolutionary party was also gathering mass support.

In 1894, Sun Yat-sen founded the

first bourgeois revolutionary society - the Society for Regenerating China. In 1904, the Society for the Revival and Restoration of China was established. In 1905, the Chinese Revolutionary Alliance was established in Tokyo. Its political platform was "to expel the Tatar barbarians and to revive Zhonghua, to establish a republic, and to distribute land equally among the people". It fought fierce battles against the bourgeois reformists and set up revolutionary organizations both at home and abroad. It launched many armed revolts, preparing the way for the Revolution of 1911.

In 1911, the Qing government gave away the right to build railways to foreign enterprises, a decision which caused widespread anger among Chinese people. The Qing Dynasty was obviously in terminal decline. The revolutionaries were about to launch an uprising in Wuhan.

Wuhan was located in the middle reaches of the Yangtze River; it was the second largest city in China after Shanghai. It was also the area with the conflict was most intense between the revolutionaries and the anti-revolution party.

On September 14, 1911, with the support of the Chinese Revolutionary Alliance, the Literary Society and the Co-progress Society entered the anti-Qing alliance, thus establishing a united front which could drive forward the uprising. They decided to launch the uprising on October 10. However, the activity of the revolutionaries aroused the attention of the Qing court. The Governors-general of Hunan and Hubei held a meeting to discuss defence on October 3, and decided to impose martial law. Since the Qing army was well prepared and the major leader of the Chinese Revolutionary Alliance Huang Xing couldn't get to Wuhan, the uprising was temporarily postponed.

On October 9, an explosion occurred unexpectedly when a revolutionary called Sun Wu was making bombs. This shocked the government. The Qing government began to arrest the revolutionaries. Given these new circumstances, the revolutionary forces in Wuchang decided to take action immediately.

On the evening of October 10, the soldiers of the revolutionary army met with the military officers who were supposed to suppress the revolution. Facilitated by the collaboration, the revolutionaries attacked and occupied the armoury at Chuwangtai, launching the Wuchang Uprising. The revolutionary army fired at the yamun of the governor-general. After a night of fierce fighting, the revolutionary army occupied Wuchang and established the Hubei Military Government on October 11. On October 12-13, the revolutionary army also occupied Hanyang and Hankou. Thus, the three towns of Wuhan were all occupied by the revolutionary army.

After the success of the Wuchang Uprising, many provinces in China responded quickly. Within two months, 14 provinces including Hubei, Hunan, Shaanxi and Jiangxi had declared independence. The Qing Dynasty rapidly disintegrated.

Sun Yat-sen returned to China in December and was recommended as temporary president at a meeting attended by representatives of 17 provinces. He was sworn in as president in Nanjing on January 1, 1912 and established the provisional government of the Republic of China. On February 12, the Qing emperor was forced to abdicate. The rule of the Qing Dynasty had ended. However, under imperial and foreign feudal pressure, Sun Yat-sen was forced to resign in April and the cunning Yuan Shikai became leader.

The Revolution of 1911 overthrew the Qing government and the feudal monarchy which had lasted for more than 2,000 years in China. China entered into a new historical stage.

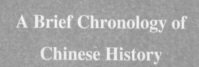

A Brief Chronology of Chinese History

Xia Dynasty	c. 2070 BC–1600 BC
Shang Dynasty	1600 BC–1046 BC
Western Zhou Dynasty	1046 BC–771 BC
Eastern Zhou Dynasty	770 BC–256 BC
Spring and Autumn Period	770 BC–476 BC
Warring States Period	475 BC–221 BC
Qin Dynasty	221 BC–206 BC
Western Han Dynasty	206 BC–25 AD
Eastern Han Dynasty	25–220
Three Kingdoms Period	220–280
Western Jin Dynasty	265–316
Eastern Jin Dynasty	317–420
Northern and Southern Dynasties	386–589
Sui Dynasty	581–618